THE PISCOPO TAPES

JOE PISCOPO

AND PAM NORRIS

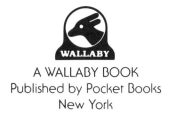

A WALLABY BOOK
Published by Pocket Books
New York

The material contained in this book is entirely the product of the authors' imaginations and has not been endorsed or approved by any person, firm or entity that is the subject of the authors' parodies and satires.

Another *Original* publication of WALLABY BOOKS

A Wallaby Book published by
POCKET BOOKS, a division of Simon & Schuster, Inc.
1230 Avenue of the Americas, New York, N.Y. 10020

ISBN: 0-671-50855-5

First Wallaby Books printing November, 1984

10   9   8   7   6   5   4   3   2   1

Designed by Jonette Jakobson

WALLABY and colophon are registered trademarks
of Simon & Schuster, Inc.

Printed in the U.S.A.

THE
PISCOPO
TAPES

For Nance, Joey, Allstar, Kanga and Rue

ACKNOWLEDGMENTS

Photography: **Christopher Little**

Additional photography: **Mark Mullen**

...e's hair and wigs were styled by **Annette Bianco.**

...e's costumes were designed by **Mark Klein.**

...e's makeup was created by **Kevin Haney.**

Graphic Art Director: **Bob Pook**

Graphic Art: **Douglas J. Zider**

Art Research: **Edd Hall**

Crossword puzzle invented by **John Debellis.**

...pecial thanks go to **Rich Piscopo,** brother and pal, for putting this whole book together; ...etsy Little; **Louis Livan** of **Purdy Optical;** the **Beanstalk Restaurant,** my office; and, ...f course, to **Eddie Murphy** for his permission to use his pictures.

" Me with Pam Norris and the pencil and paper used to write the book."

INTRODUCTION

This book is dedicated to the people whose very existence made it possible: Andy Rooney, Joan Rivers, David Hartman, Lee Iacocca, Ed McMahon, Jerry Lewis, Ted Koppel, Phil Donahue, David Letterman and Frank Sinatra. It is only because of their distinctive personal styles that I can make a fine living making fun of them. Without them, I would be forced to do imitations of my Uncle Lou from Pennsylvania, who is pretty funny but not as well known. He sounds like this: "Hey Joey!" (Right now, I'm squinching up my face, making my eyes pop out and my chin disappear. I look just like Uncle Lou, only more so.) "A branch fell off the tree in the backyard! Let's go out and look at it!" (Now I'm pulling my shirt sideways and putting the buttons in the wrong buttonholes. For some reason, Lou never gets his shirt buttoned right, and Aunt Claire is always bugging him about it.) "There's a big game today with the Nittamy Lions!" (Another joke. Lou is a big fan of Penn State's Nittany Lions, but after all these years, he still gets the name wrong. This is a running gag in our family.) Anyway, this is a dead-on impersonation of Uncle Lou, and if you knew him, I guarantee you'd be dying. However, as you can see, it doesn't really work if you don't know the guy. That's the difference between Uncle Lou and Frank Sinatra. Sure, there are other differences — for example, they have different jobs and live in different states — but that's the main one, for the purposes of this book.

I have had the great pleasure of working with some of the people "interviewed" in this book. Others, I have been fortunate enough to meet with and talk to. A few have taken the trouble to playfully call my lawyers. To me, this proves, once again, that the bigger they are, the nicer they are. All of them, I know, realize that imitation is the highest form of flattery. To have their speaking style, their physical appearance and the intimate details of their personal lives picked apart and mercilessly mocked, is a tribute second only to the Congressional Medal of Honor.

I'm glad we've gotten that cleared up.

Joe Piscopo

As the editors of Joe's first book, we are very proud of The Piscopo Tapes. *This book is witty, charming, and takes a wonderfully affectionate poke at the celebrities who have become a part of our lives. We fully believe that Joe is one of the greatest comics of our time.*

We must inform you, however, that we have no permission whatsoever to use the magazine titles or their trademarks that are parodied in this book, and, obviously, we have no permission from the celebrities whose likenesses Joe recreated. In fact, we told Joe that we would not be responsible for anything he said or did. Ever. These "interviews" are entirely false. The characters depicted never uttered a word of what you see here.

You did a great job, Joe, but business is business.

TV GUIDE

Local, Network and Cable/Pay Listings

The Toughest Nice Guy On TV Donahue

TV Executives Who Care About Quality

The Earth Is Flat

The Upcoming Season Promises Fresh, Original, and Well-Written Shows

"What do you *think?* Help me out here!"

TV Guide turns the tables on TV's top interviewer

Politicians stammer, spokespeople sputter and public figures shrivel before the microphones of TV's toughest interviewer: Phil Donahue. As relentless as Mike Wallace, and as probing as Sam Donaldson, Phil Donahue is a formidable questioner. TV Guide *wondered: What if the shoe were on the other foot? Would that foot end up in his mouth? We set out to interview Phil Donahue, using some of his own notorious techniques.*

TV GUIDE: First of all, let me welcome you, Mr. Donahue.

DONAHUE: Thank you. It's very nice to be…

TV GUIDE: Oh, come off it! Isn't that just the same small talk we've all heard before? What do you *really* think?

DONAHUE: About what?

TV GUIDE: The whole thing. All these world problems. How would you solve them?

DONAHUE: Well, I believe that the world's problems could be solved if we could all just sit down and talk to each other.

TV GUIDE: All of us? Okay. Question. Mr. Donahue, there are well over six billion people in the world. How could all of us sit down and talk to each other? Where would we get that many chairs?

DONAHUE: It's possible.

TV GUIDE: Mr. Donahue, there is no banquet room at any Holiday Inn in the world that could accommodate that many people. And supposing, just for the sake of argument, that you could find a big enough meeting hall. When would you schedule this meeting-cum-conference? It's hard enough to set up a simple lunch date with, for example, Heather Locklear. How can you find a date when all six billion of us are free? I myself am a busy man.

DONAHUE: Some Sunday afternoon. Nobody ever does anything on Sunday afternoons.

TV GUIDE: I guess that would be possible. We could serve a simple brunch, scrambled eggs or something.

DONAHUE: With that many people, we're going to *have* to keep it simple.

Scrambled eggs, Bloody Marys, toast and coffee.

TV GUIDE: I don't know if this is really a feasible plan, Mr. Donahue. How can you possibly serve all those people? After all, if everybody in the world is invited, that means all the *waiters* in the world are invited. Ergo, you will have no one to serve the food!

DONAHUE: I think the thing to do would be just to set up a buffet, and let everyone serve themselves. We'll make the coffee ahead of time, and bring it in aboard tanker ships.

TV GUIDE: Mr. Donahue, this plan is preposterous. If one uses all the tanker ships in the world to bring in *coffee,* how will you transport the Bloodies?

DONAHUE: Hmmm. Your point is well taken. Okay. Screwdrivers. We go to the reservoir and dump in ten or twelve tons of frozen concentrated orange juice, and a thousand barrels of vodka! And we keep it all backed up behind Hoover Dam until everyone comes over at eleven o'clock.

TV GUIDE: It'll never work. Eleven o'clock? Who's going to get up that early on a Sunday morning?

DONAHUE: We'll make it noon. And we'll call it the "World Brunch for Peace."

TV GUIDE: I suppose *I'll* have to do all the cleaning up.

DONAHUE: Nah. Marlo and the other girls will do it.

TV GUIDE: Don't you think you ought to ask your wife first?

DONAHUE: What for? You know, this global brunch is a great idea. So many of the world's problems are caused by a lack of honest, open communication. Like the war between Iran and Iraq. They are so close to each other, yet they have never had the courage to *be* close to each other. To open up. Instead, they've suppressed their feelings so long that all that pent-up hostility just builds and builds. They need to *express* that hostility.

TV GUIDE: Doesn't bombing each other and using nerve gas and blowing each other up count as "expressing hostility"?

DONAHUE: Not really. What they really need to do, what would be *really* radical, would be if they just had the courage to say, "Hey. It really *bugs* me that you invade my space and try to kill all my people." Hate and love are very close, as you know. Oftentimes, a country will bomb another country just because it's too embarrassed to say, "I love you."

TV GUIDE: Interesting. You're very expressive yourself, physically as well as verbally, particularly when you're interviewing. Most interviewers just sit there, but you've got a number of interview positions. Could you show us some of them?

DONAHUE: Sure. My big one is "The Dive." You start by standing in the aisle, feet apart, holding your microphone in your right hand, like this. Then you spot someone in the middle of a row, who looks like she has a question to ask. Bend the knees, spring into the air, extend the right arm, and dive horizontally across the row, ending with the microphone under her nose, arm fully extended.

"THE DIVE"

TV GUIDE: You'll certainly never see Lesley Stahl doing that one!

DONAHUE: Well, the Dive is a questioning posture. There are some listening postures, as well. "The Arm-Head-Drape" is my signature listening posture.

TV GUIDE: Could you demonstrate?

DONAHUE: Certainly. Okay, you're listening to someone, which is always fairly boring, and the Arm-Head-Drape let's them know it. The microphone goes in the right hand, since you're not using it. Raise your right arm vertically, elbow next to your right ear. Then bend the right arm so that the right forearm rests on your head like a hat. Relax the left wrist and dangle hand.

TV GUIDE: That certainly gets your message across. You're bored!

DONAHUE: You'll never see Ted Koppel doing this during an interview. He suppresses everything, I think.

TV GUIDE: One difference between you and the other interviewers is that you interview mostly women. Do you feel you have a special rapport with the fairer sex?

DONAHUE: There's an interview position that establishes immediate "rapport," if you get my meaning, with the women. While they're answering

"THE ARM-HEAD DRAPE"

"THE PHALLIC POSE"

14

"THE HUNCH AND STALK"

photo by Christopher Little

my question, I drop my hand mike down to—shall we say—below waist level. It reminds the girls of who's still the boss.

TV GUIDE: What if you really don't like what your interviewee is saying, personally?

DONAHUE: Well, I'm a journalist, and my job is to solicit information, not express my personal opinions on everything. But there are subtle ways to communicate your feelings. If someone says something you disagree with, you can do what I do sometimes, turn around and run away as fast as I can.

TV GUIDE: Subtle.

DONAHUE: You're standing in the aisle, and he's in the middle of a sentence. You turn abruptly on your heel, hunch up your shoulders to cover your ears, and stalk away real fast. That usually surprises 'em! Hey, where are you going? I'm not finished!

(Ed. note: The turning of the tables was complete. We pulled the Hunch and Stalk on Phil. Did he like it? Not much!)

television crossword

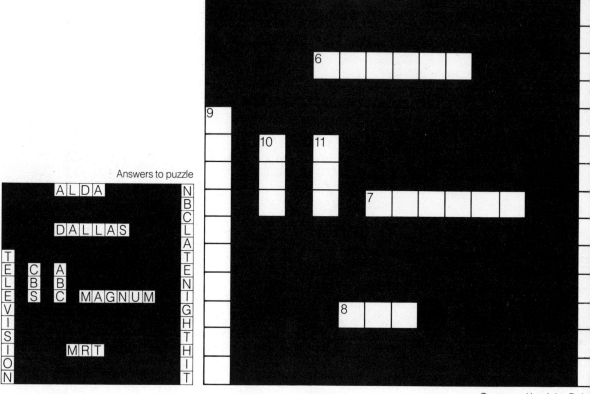

Answers to puzzle

Crossword by John Deb...

down

5 NBC late night hit
9 Televison
10 CBS
11 ABC

across

1 Alda
6 Dallas
7 Magnum
8 Mr. T

COSMOPOLITAN

Mr. Rooney Goes to Cosmo! Our First Male Cover–Boy Ever Tells All!

Men Behind Bars: How to Make Time with Dreamy Guys Who Are Serving Time

Delivery Boys: Piping Hot and Right at Your Door!

Talking About Orgasms at Cocktail Parties

Unemployed Heroin Addicts: Don't Rule Them Out!

One Girls Steamy Experiences with the Classified Ads! How She Finally Sold That Sofa

Do You Like Anything in Pants? (Good For You) A Quiz

Your Sister's Husband: Is He Off-Limits?

A few *Sensuous* minutes

Imagine *this,* darling girl! You're cuddled up in your delectable boudoir on a Sunday evening, ready for some *excitement,* but (sigh!) *alone!* Suddenly, five *devastating* men appear (as if by magic!) before you, and they spend the next hour teasing you with racy stories, *provoking* you with sly (and spicy!) suggestions, and finally (when you can't stand it another *minute*) baring *all!* Then, they slip away (just as magically!), leaving you titillated, bemused, but oh so satisfied.

Did you think we were talking about sex? *Silly* girl! That sixty minutes of ecstasy is, of course, "60 Minutes," that simply scrumptious television show that's as revealing as your naughtiest nightie (tee-hee). Those five fascinating man-creatures are Mike Wallace, Morley Safer, Harry Reasoner, Ed Bradley and (save the most *huggable* for last!) Andy Rooney. This grumpy old (sensuous!) grouch isn't easily satisfied, but maybe *you* could turn him on – and we *don't* mean turning on the *television!* Olé!

ROONEY: Pardon me, madam, but can we start the interview now?
COSMO: Impatient (impetuous!) boy! How *can* we deny you? But if we *start* too *fast,* you might not be a "60-Minute" man (giggle)!
ROONEY: Huh?
COSMO: Never mind. Okay. "What do you like in bed?"
ROONEY: Pillows. The big fluffy kind. But not *too* big. If the pillow is too big, it holds your head up too high and mashes your chin into your chest. Especially if the pillow is filled with foam rubber. Did you ever notice that foam rubber pillows smell like old tires? I don't want to sleep with my head on an old tire. And why do they call it *foam* rubber? Was it foamy once? And did they dip it out of a big vat? I bet it *really* smelled bad *then.*
COSMO: That's not exactly what we meant....
ROONEY: The only thing worse than a foam rubber pillow is one of those flat, heavy ones. I don't know *what's* in those. It's not feathers and it's not foam rubber. It's real hard and it feels like a

with *Andy Rooney*

folded-up sheet. Maybe it *is* a folded-up sheet. I don't know.

COSMO: What we were really trying to ask was: What do you like to *do* in bed?

ROONEY: Eat sunflower seeds. Except I don't know what to do with the shells. Of course, I suppose I could buy them already shelled. But it doesn't seem right. Abe Lincoln would have shelled his *own* sunflower seeds. Of course, Abe Lincoln may have never eaten sunflower seeds at all. I don't know. But he definitely didn't eat sunflower seeds in bed while watching reruns of "The People's Court" late at night.

COSMO: Let me put this question another way. . . .

ROONEY: Anyway, what happens if you lose on "The People's Court"? Do you have to go to "The People's Prison"?

COSMO: Okay. Let's put it this way. A lissome lovely has invited you to a daytime dalliance (*quelle scandale!*) at a quiet hotel. What is the first thing you do when you reach the supersexy scene?

ROONEY: Probably look for the ice machine. I like hotels that have one on every floor. That way you don't have to walk around carrying a slippery plastic bucket. And why do they put the ice bucket in the bathroom? I'm not going to have a cocktail party in the bathroom. Of course, the glasses are in there, too. Sealed for your protection. What does that mean, anyway? It's just some Saran Wrap stretched over the top of the glass. What would happen if a glass wasn't "sealed for my protection"? Would it blow up or something? They don't say. Of course, the toilet seat is sealed for your protection, too, with that little paper band. Apparently, hotel bathrooms are pretty dangerous places, what with all the glasses and toilet seats that you have to be protected from. And why are those little bars of soap always either Camay or Cashmere Bouquet? Is somebody getting paid off?

COSMO: But, *outside* the bathroom?

ROONEY: You mean, the bedroom?

COSMO: Yes, yes, YES!!

ROONEY: I don't like it. First of all, the bed is always the wrong height. I don't think I know how high my bed is at home, but if I get into a bed that's a different height, I don't like it. Also, at some hotels, they put a chocolate on your pillow. I don't want food all over my pillow. It's lumpy and if it melts during the night, I wake up with my hair full of chocolate. Sometimes I think those hotel managers are just plain stupid.

COSMO: But why don't you *eat* that tempting sweet (before you go to bed with *your* sweetie!)?

ROONEY: Eat it? Just what I want: to go to sleep with my teeth full of candy. Some hotels even put a matchbook on the pillow. I can't stand them. Of course, it's not the matchbooks that are so bad. It's the people who collect them. Don't you hate it when people take matchbooks from *every* place they've ever been, then bring them home and put them in a brandy snifter? Then they put the brandy snifter on the coffee table. Then they pick out a matchbook and tell you some long, boring story about some boring hotel they stayed in. And then they brag about how the hotel had an indoor swimming pool. Did you ever notice how dirty indoor swimming pools always are? I guess that's because you usually find them at the YMCA. They always seem to have a head on them. And they smell bad. Maybe that's where they get foam rubber from. Anyway, they're pretty dirty. Of course, the whole city's pretty dirty, too. Did you ever notice how people are always complaining about how dirty the city is? But when you think about it, there's much *more* dirt out in the country. Because of all the farming, it's necessary.

COSMO: *Speaking* of dirt, *we* want the dirt on your oh-so-scrupulous "60 Minutes" guys! Are they really as "straightlaced" as they appear, or would they be willing to do a little investigative reporting...*undercover*...if you know what I mean!!

ROONEY: Actually, they're pretty boring guys. Mike, Harry and Ed are okay. Morley Safer has two names I never heard of, so I guess that's kind of interesting. Did you ever notice that on "60 Minutes," I'm the comic relief? That pretty much sums it up.

COSMO: Well, back to sex.

ROONEY: Is that what we were talking about?

COSMO: You're a man who notices every little (teensy!) thing! What mortal maiden could *possibly* please this picayune pundit?!

ROONEY: What?

COSMO: Do you have groupies?

ROONEY: Did you ever notice that if *anyone's* on TV long enough, he will eventually get some fans? The Fonz did it. Bill Bixby did it. The only person who was on TV for years and years, but never had any fans, was Bonnie Franklin. No one knows how she did it. Sure, I have groupies. Some are tall. Some are short. Most of them are girls. I'm glad.

COSMO: What do they want you to do?

ROONEY: Usually they just want to hear me say "Did you ever notice..." and then start complaining about something insignificant. They love it. They can't get enough of it. Some women just like curmudgeons. That's what I am. Of course, it's just because I'm a celebrity, that they like it. If their husbands sat around the living room and complained about *every* little thing, they probably wouldn't like it.

COSMO: Do you comply with their (wicked!) wishes?

ROONEY: Well, usually if I run into some fans, I just complain to make them happy. I'll say, "Did you ever notice how obnoxious autograph-hounds are?" That thrills them. I don't know why. Then I sign my autograph and they go away.

COSMO: Playing hard to get! You sly boy! Now, let's talk about sex. Have you ever delivered a humorous speech about the female orgasm?

ROONEY: Sure. But never on TV.

COSMO: Can we coax you into a little X-rated extemporation?

ROONEY: Did you ever notice how everyone talks about orgasms? It's in magazines. It's on TV. Even people standing in line at fast-food places talk about it. I try not to listen. It used to be that psychologists said there were three kinds of orgasms. Vaginal. Clitoral. And fake.

COSMO: Go on.

ROONEY: This is too embarrassing. What kind of magazine are you running over here?

COSMO: Well, our typical reader is actually a bit like you. Our (original!) word for it is *mouseburger*. That's a depressing Midwesterner with minimal talent but an annoying persistence and a big chip on the shoulder; someone who thinks that life is *easy* for other people but oh-so-(horrors!) *difficult* for them!

ROONEY: I guess you could call me that *Cosmopolitan* girl. 🐱

Amos 'n Andy

PLAYBOY

ENTERTAINMENT FOR MEN

SPECIAL GUEST
PLAYMATE
OF THE MONTH

THE
BEAUTIFUL
JOAN RIVERS

The Beautiful Joan Rivers

CAN A WOMAN be both funny and sexy at the same time? Our Mi? November has the answer. "Sexy? Me? Aaaaaaugh!" sk replies, sticking a slender finger provocatively down he throat. Retching noises come from between her moist an parted lips. "Grow up! You know who does my makeup? Sherwir Williams! We're talking Cover the World! Look at these *bags* unde my eyes! I should get twist-ties with these! I'm a dog! Arf! Arf!"

Who is our mysterious lady of the laughs? She's the gag-goddess that Johnny Carson has handpicked to keep his seat warm — and her gatefold may heat up other parts of his anatomy as well! "Ohhh! Get real!" is Miss Joan Rivers's response to that waggish speculation. But we beg to differ, and that's no joke.

It seems that every curvaceous and stunning Playmate we interview always insists that she never thought of herself as attractive. But few insist on it with the fervor and volubility of Joan. "Can we talk? I'm telling you, I'm a dog! I'm not exactly young, either — Edgar keeps giving me Cycle 4! And this hair? Is that a natural color? It looks like I stole it off a mannequin at Bamberger's when the floor manager was looking the other way! You know who does my hair? Lawn Doctor!" quips the *femme* both *fatale* and *funnie*. Obviously, the gently rolling Rivers does not believe that she herself is both sexy and funny.

But if our jaunty Joan doesn't believe that all her

punch lines are firmly in place (as we can attest!), why did she consent to do our pictorial? "I saw what you did with Joan Collins last year. I figured if you could make that old bag look good, you could do anything. Grow up! You turned back her odometer about 50,000 miles! Did you shoot that pictorial in soft-focus, or did the San Francisco fog roll into your studio by accident? Grow up! You would have needed a lighthouse to find her in those pictures! I've heard of shooting through cheesecloth, but that looked like you were shooting through shag carpeting! What did you air brush those pictures with — a Hoover?" Ms. Collins, we protested, got the same treatment as all our other lovely Playmates. "Yeah, I've heard about you guys and how you tape everything up and back, and the pink lights and the ice cubes and the elastic straps," the bubbling Rivers riposted. "It's about as sexy as being in a full body cast. Let's just get it over with," squealed the eager jokestress.

Unlike our average gatefold, Joan is a married lady and she insisted that her husband, Edgar, be present during the shooting of her pictorial. "Not really for moral support," said Joan, "I just want Edgar to see me naked once." Edgar, however, announced that he had suddenly remembered an important previous engagement at his chiropodist, and left, but not before telling us that *he* definitely thought Joan was as sexy as she was funny.

And so, Joan Rivers is our Miss November, and it looks like it's going to be a hot one. How does Joan feel about following in the footsteps of so many other legendary beauties who have bared all for our delighted lens? "Bo Derek? She's in your magazine a lot, isn't she? I think it's kind of sweet that she and her husband have this little Mom-and-Pop business — her breasts. Whatever happened to Barbi Benton? Talk about talent! There was a girl who aspired to be Lynda Carter and couldn't quite make it! I call that pathetic!" Joan yells, sympathetically.

Of course, there's no danger of *this* Rivers's highwater mark dropping — her popularity continues unabated, and Joan hopes her gatefold will win her even more fans. "Edgar says my naked body is just like a *Playboy* centerfold," explains our Ms. Joan. "It's flat and wrinkled."

We couldn't agree more. And now, "Can we *peek*?"

photo by Troy Miller

25

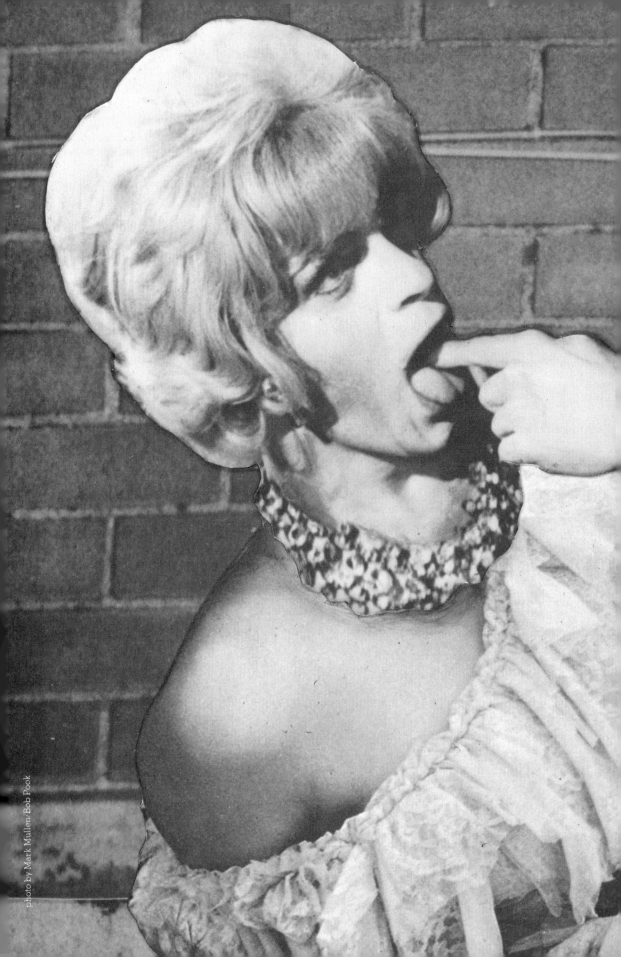

"I think being feminine is all the little things you do to keep yourself dainty and delicate. Like shaving your armpits! Yes, Christina Onassis, I'm talking about you! It looks like you're trying to smuggle two Brillo pads through customs! Grow up! The woman could wear Velcro dress shields!"

PLAYMATE DATA SHEET

photo by Mark Mullen/Bob Pook

NAME: _Joan Rivers_

BUST: _Oh please! I have no chest! We're talking concave! I can lie in bed and eat cereal out of it!_

WAIST: _Grow up! I don't have a waist! I have a red line around my middle where the pantyhose are too tight! That's it!_

HIPS: _Hips I have. I told Edgar that a lot of famous women have done centerfolds, and that I was bringing up the rear. He said I better do it before I do the centerfold._

HEIGHT: _5'5"_   WEIGHT: _Somewhere between Karen and Liz._

BIRTH DATE: _Make me laugh._

BIRTHPLACE: _I have a feeling I was not a wanted child. My mother didn't go to a hospital. She gave birth by means of a low Heimlich maneuver._

AMBITIONS: _To be a successful entertainer and to help bring peace to the world._

TURN-ONS: _Thinking of new ways to call people fat, going to the furrier, people who believe you when you say you're "in your forties."_

TURN-OFFS: _Having varicose veins stripped at a While-U-Wait place, people who say you're anorexic._

FAVORITE FOODS: _Celery, boiled water, ice cubes, Perrier, gum._

FAVORITE BOOKS: _"1001 Humorous Anecdotes for Toastmasters"; "Libel Statutes for the State of California"._

IDEAL EVENING: _To host the "Tonight" show with guests Victoria Principal, Linda Evans, Angie Dickinson, and Shelley Winters injected with sodium pentothal truth serum._

SECRET FANTASY: _For Liz to get married and gain weight._

Forbes

CHRYSLER'S LEE IACOCCA

IN AN AMERICAN-MADE INTERVIEW

ALSO: FORBES RANKS THE TOP
100 COMPANIES 12 DIFFERENT WAYS

INCLUDING ALPHABETICALLY AND
BY THE NUMBER OF LETTERS
IN THEIR NAMES

THE IMPORTANCE OF BEING NON-IMPORTED AN INTERVIEW WITH CHRYSLER'S LEE IACOCCA

Ask the average man in the street to name the chief executive officers of the nation's top five hundred companies, and chances are he will only be able to come up with fifty or sixty — and you better choose the street carefully, at that. Outside of Wall Street, the number drops even further. Such is the average American's ignorance of the corporate chiefs who shape his very destiny, thank God. But one chief executive officer has become something of a popular icon (perhaps we should say "iacoccon"), and that is Chrysler's Lee Iacocca. Iacocca successfully managed to snatch the company as it tottered on the brink of a financial precipice, defend it from legions of snarling creditors and bravely battle it back into marketing position in a stormy and terrifying economic climate, eventually winning the hero's laurels of financial and technical success. Okay, maybe we're dramatizing this a little. What do you want us to say in these articles about executives? That they're a bunch of guys in gray suits who sit behind desks and move papers around, and that they all seem to be named George? Forget it.

The following is an interview with Iacocca conducted at Chrysler headquarters in Michigan.

Hello, Mr. Iacocca.
LEE: Please, call me Lee.

Hello, Lee. Thank you for agreeing to have lunch with us.
LEE: No problem. There's a saying in the business community: "Let's have lunch." Basically, it means, "Let's get together and talk turkey about our fine American-made products."

Is that what it means?
LEE: Sure! And I'm just bursting with real honest-to-gosh Yankee pride right now. Do you know what about?

What?
LEE: This!

Aaaaaaa!
LEE: What's the matter?

I'm sorry. It looks like a piece of dead brain.
LEE: Close. What it actually is, is a piece of particularly exotic sushi. *Japanese* sushi. And you're right, it's disgusting. Now tell me something. Would you like to drive down the street in this?

In that?
LEE: Is this what you want to strap the luggage to, pile the kids in, and drive to Grandma's house?

No?
LEE: Darn tooting! Because you're an American, am I right?

Actually, I'm from Jersey.
LEE: Really? I have a vacation home in Jersey, near Piscataway. That's God's country! But we were talking about the driving experience.

Right.
LEE: Let me put it to you another way. Suppose you were all dressed up in the morning, feeling as fresh as an American-made daisy, and ready to go to work. You go out into your driveway — and you have to climb into a big pile of sauerkraut, and fight the freeway traffic in *that!* All right, it may be an extremely well-*engineered* pile of sauerkraut, but you still come to work with cabbage juice in your hair! Do you get my meaning?

I think so. What you're saying is that it would be preferable to go out to your garage and find a big juicy burger.
LEE: Exactly! A big fragrant American-made burger that could handle the curves, meet federal emission standards, and fulfill your protein needs! With ketchup and mustard *standard.*

What about the pickle slice?
LEE: That's the sunroof.

But wouldn't the lower bun be a less-than-ideal driving surface, just from the viewpoint of traction?

LEE: Now you're just being silly. You know what we're talking about.

Sorry.
LEE: Picture this. It's a beautiful American-made morning. Thousands of American auto workers pour into a building, and get on line. Do you know where we are?

The unemployment office?
LEE: No! The Chrysler factory! The Big Four American car manufacturers all have their headquarters in Detroit, the Motor City.

Motown.
LEE: Right! And believe me, the Jackson Five and the Big Four have plenty in common besides the Motown label! Both of us have been together for a long time, turning out successes for the American public. They had innovative break-dance choreography; we had innovative brake-shoe design. We have glove compartments; Michael wears a glove. Sure, we had the Edsel, but they had Jermaine's solo career.

You had the Pinto; they had Michael's hair.
LEE: You get the idea! Anyway, you wouldn't accuse the Jacksons of poor management and outdated production techniques, would you?

I guess not....
LEE: Then you can't accuse American car manufacturers, either!

This is a little confusing.
LEE: I'm a car salesman, remember?

Right. Well, your logic aside, I must admit that you have certainly turned Chrysler around financially, since its near-bankruptcy a few years ago. At that time,

31

you received massive government-backed loans.

LEE: Well, they weren't *that* big.

I have the figures here. The amount of the federally guaranteed loans came to one million jillion zillion krillion dollars.

LEE: Anyway, we paid it all back.

Out of profits from sales of Chryslers?

LEE: Partially. We also had bake sales and a dance-a-thon to raise money. Begging on the streets was also a source of some revenues. But part of the money came from car sales, yes.

How did you go about increasing sales?

LEE: We improved gas mileage and design and lowered the price. Mostly, however, it was a marketing victory, and, in all modesty, I feel that I can take the credit.

How so?

LEE: My background is in marketing. A few years back, when Chrysler was losing money out the tailpipe, its commercials were no good. Most of them featured a shapely girl lying on the hood of an automobile. No one looked at the car. Then *I* started doing the commercials myself. Frankly, I'm no glamor-boy. Next to my face, the front grille of a Chrysler LeBaron looked pretty attractive.

Ingenious.

LEE: And most importantly, *I* was made in America! Remember when Ricardo Montalban did the ads for Chrysler Cordoba? They didn't work. You know why?

Because Ricardo was not made in America?

LEE: Exactly. He's Spanish, I think. Tell me, if you had an important date and really wanted to impress a girl, would you drive up to her door in a big bowl of gazpacho? Enough said!

I'll go along with that. ■

PARIS MATCH

LE JERRY MAGNIFIQUE:

Un conversation en anglaise avec le maître de comédie

Plus de remarques insultées pour les touristes Américains

Escargots et les jambes de frogs: Vraimente, ils sont disgustants!

Jerry Lewis est l'homme plus wackie dans le monde.

═══ Hi! Hi! ═══

*(The following interview is a translation
from PARIS MATCH magazine of a conversation between
Joe Piscopo and Jerry Lewis.)*

**The American comedic man of the name Joseph Piscopo
donates to us this interview with the great
Jerry Lewis, funny and silly fellow superb.
They are both very much to laugh,
do you not think so?**

JOE: Hi, Jerry.

JERRY: And it's absolutely wonderful to *be* here. Let me embarrass this man for a minute. Joe, Joe, Joe. I know comedy and you are comedy.

JOE: Jerry, you write, you produce, you direct, you act. You're world famous, considered by many a cinematic genius, and you've been making movies for thirty years. Yet you have never won a single Academy Award.

JERRY: Joe, as you know, the Hollywood community has never been hospitable to genius. Orson Welles, Charlie Chaplin, myself: We were all better appreciated in Europe. Life is not easy for the artist who is ahead of his time.

JOE: So you think perhaps you were too sophisticated; above the audience's heads?

JERRY: What? I can't hear you; I've got chopsticks in my

ears! (And indeed, Jerry did have chopsticks in his ears, and up his nose as well. When our startled Japanese waiter approached the table, Lewis broke into his famous Japanese routine from The Geisha Boy.)
JERRY: TONG TING SHUNG HONG!

JOE: Ha ha. The Geisha Boy. That was a wonderful film.
JERRY: They'll never make them like that again.

JOE: Which recent movies have you found to be the funniest of the lot?
JERRY: On Golden Pond was great. I cracked up when the guy pretended to have a heart attack, then sat up and went, "Ha! Ha!" Of course, I did it first. That's an old routine of mine.
(At this point, Jerry grabbed his heart and dived for the floor, landing at the feet of our startled waiter, who helped Jerry back into his chair.)

WAITER: Here, have some water.
JERRY: Thank you.

JOE: So, tell me, Jerry. Your part in King of Comedy, the Martin Scorsese film, was a completely straight dramatic role, and you were triumphant in it. Since then, have you been offered more roles that show off the new, serious Jerry?
JERRY: Well, one...
(And water pours out of Jerry's mouth, soaking his immaculate shirtfront! He had been holding a mouthful, waiting for his opportunity to make the gag, and I had been a willing sucker.)

JOE: Ha ha. I guess that answers my question.
JERRY: Actually, Joe, I have been offered many serious dramatic parts.

JOE: Oh, forgive me.
JERRY: As a matter of fact, I was offered the lead in Silkwood.

JOE: You were going to play Karen Silkwood?
JERRY: Well, the movie would have been slightly different. The character of Karen Silkwood would have been changed to a fellow named Melvin Porchnik.

JOE: You.
JERRY: That's right. Anyway, Melvin is a goofy guy who works with nuclear wastes, and sure enough, he accidentally takes some home. Before he knows it, his boss and the government are after him!

JOE: What was the title?
JERRY: The Nutty Nuclear Worker. It was classic comedy. Ended with a hilarious car chase.

JOE: Sounds great.
JERRY: Joe, I think it would have been my Oscar.

JOE: But you did recently win induction into the French Legion of Honor. That's quite an achievement.
JERRY: Mais, sacré bleu, ce n'est une libnon verculaire de pouf de vise!

JOE: I beg your pardon!
JERRY: Sounds just like French, doesn't it? Joe, I tell you, I went to France and they couldn't tell the difference. Yes, I won the Legion of Honor, and I hope to win it again next year, and again and again. But monsieur, your coat is verree dirtee! (Now, Jerry begins brushing off my jacket vigorously, managing to "accidentally" pull my tie off, as he goes into his famous "valet" routine from The Bell Hop.)

JOE: Ha ha. So let's talk about the early days. Do you ever miss Dean?
JERRY: Well, Dean and I have gone our separate ways. I went on to become a world-famous cinematic genius and humanitarian. He went on to work with the Golddiggers. And the man never works on an empty liver. Which is the better path?

JOE: Gee. That's hard to say.
JERRY: You're joking, of course. I myself take an occasional social drink, but never to the point of losing control. (Jerry takes a sip of his drink.) Aahh! (His face contorting, Jerry grabbed his throat as if he was choking. After some heavy breathing, he finally seemed to catch his breath.) Hey, sweetie pie, this interview is starting to bore me.
(Sure enough, Jerry had fallen into his Buddy Love character from The Nutty Professor. But he soon

returned to normal.)
JOE: Ha ha.
JERRY: See, I made you laugh. And that, my friend, is the nature of the dramatic art we call comedy. To elicit a laugh from one of one's fellow men, to somehow make the intellectual connection between man's absurdity and the futility of his rational efforts to overcome that absurdity—to alleviate some of the suffering in the world by simply accepting its chaotic nature...well, let me put it this way. La La LA LA LA! *(Jerry crosses his eyes and bucks out his teeth, and suddenly he is the beloved "nine-year-old boy.")* Oh, you're a nice man, Mr. Piscopo! La la la la la! *(At this point, Jerry puts the tape recorder on his head, wraps the microphone cord around his face, and sticks the mike up his nose, effectively ending the interview.)* ■

Reader's Digest

GOOD MORNING AMERICA'S DAVID HARTMAN
PAGE 15

TRAPPED!
TWO PEOPLE ABANDONED AT AN EXTREMELY BAD PLAY, BUT THEY KNOW SOMEONE IN THE CAST....
PAGE 61

HAVE YOU A HUMOROUS ANECDOTE? ARE YOU SURE?
PAGE 4

ANIMAL PROSTITUTION: THE SHAME OF OUR NATION'S FARMERS AND BREEDERS
PAGE 32

IT'S TIME TO TAKE A STAND AGAINST MURDER
PAGE 20

UNFORGETTABLE MARVIN BABCOCK
PAGE 44

Good Morning, David A Conversation with A.M.'s Genial Host

This interview is a condensation of an in-depth fourteen-hour, six-part series of talks between late-night's Joe Piscopo and early-morning's David Hartman.

JOE: It's a pleasure to meet you, Mr. Hartman.

DAVID: Duhh...Good morning!

JOE: Good...uh...*evening.*

DAVID: Good morning! Good morning, Joe!

JOE: All right. Good morning.

DAVID: And good morning America!

JOE: Ha ha. I love that show, David.

DAVID: What show?

JOE: Your show. "Good Morning America." The early-morning news program. The first question I want to ask you is this: How do you feel it compares to the other early-morning news shows? For example, "Today."

DAVID: I didn't watch the other shows today.

JOE: No, I mean "Today." The show that's named "Today."

DAVID: They're naming a show today?

JOE: No. "Today" is the morning news.

DAVID: Oh! "The CBS Morning News"!

JOE: No. "Today" is the *NBC* morning news. "The CBS Morning News" is a different show.

DAVID: Is that the show that's going to be named today?

JOE: No. *No* show is going to be named today. Look. There are three shows, "Good Morning America."

DAVID: Good morning!

JOE: Hold on a second. Hear me out. There are three shows. "Good Morning America."

DAVID: Good morning!

JOE: "The CBS Morning News." And "Today." "Today" is on NBC.

DAVID: What channel is "The CBS Morning News" on?

JOE: CBS.

DAVID: What a coincidence!

JOE: That's the one with Diane Sawyer. She's the pretty one who used to work for Nixon.

DAVID: Oh. Did she have to go to jail?

JOE: No. She never got in trouble.

DAVID: Then how did she have twins?

JOE: You're thinking of Jane Pauley. She's the one who had the twins. On "Today."

DAVID: She had the twins right on the program? Wow!

JOE: No. She *had* the twins. But obviously, she didn't do it on the morning news!

DAVID: Of course not. Why would she do it on the "Morning News"? I'm not stupid!

JOE: Sorry.

DAVID: Diane *Sawyer* had twins on the "Morning News"! Jane Pauley had them on "Today."

JOE: Diane Sawyer doesn't have twins. She used to be a Junior Miss. Jane Pauley has twins. She's married to Garry Trudeau.

DAVID: Wow! That's impressive!

JOE: Yes, he's very good.

DAVID: But why doesn't Jane have to live in Canada with him? Wouldn't she be the queen?

JOE: He doesn't live in Canada.

DAVID: Oh, that's right. He's not prime minister anymore, is he? You know, you've got to keep right on top of foreign affairs when you're in my position. I'm very interested in them.

JOE: You are?

DAVID: Yes. That is why I gave up acting and became a journalist. I feel that in today's modern world, everyone should learn about many different lands and cultures, and their interesting ways of life.

JOE: In that case, what do you think about Central America?

DAVID: Oh, I'm very well versed in that area. I just went there on an assignment.

JOE: You must have seen a lot of action.

DAVID: I'll say! There was a corn-shucking contest, a state fair and a greased-hog race! I was born in the center of America. But ask me about a foreign country, OK?

JOE: All right. How about the Soviet Union?

DAVID: That's another name for Russia. Am I correct?

DAVID: Yes.

DAVID: Russia is a land of many contrasts. Some parts of it are cold. Other parts are warmer. The exports are minerals, machinery and other products.

JOE: You're reading your shirt cuff.

DAVID: Am not!

JOE: I'm sorry. That's very good, David.

DAVID: Thank you. Good morning!

JOE: I think that display alone answers the critics who say that you, Bryant Gumbel, and the other morning journalists don't have any background in hard news.

DAVID: That's not true. We do a lot of hard news. Half the time I don't even understand what I'm saying, it's so hard.

JOE: You're accused of glossing over the news quickly, and never analyzing in depth.

DAVID: That's not true, either, Joe. We go into subjects at great length. Last month, we did a whole week of shows about jazzerobics with lots of film of newsmakers jumping around in leotards. Then we did a whole week of analysis on exer dancing, with a lot of film. The following week, we had a special series about rhythmcizing. And this week, we're beginning an in-depth look at aeroba-boogie.

JOE: That's on today?

DAVID: No. It's on "Good Morning America."

JOE: But is it on "Good Morning," today?

DAVID: "Good Morning Today?" Is *that* the new show you were talking about?

JOE: Good-bye, David.

DAVID: Good morning?

Pe**o**ple weekly

**My oh my!
David Letterman
is shedding his
corn-fed image
and sowing a
few wild oats**

**Tank therapy
for your goldfish**

**TV's Judge Wapner
rates the
Supreme Court**

photo by Christopher Little

LATE NIGHT'S HUCK FINN HITS NEW YORK'S RITZY WATERING HOLES, AS THE EMCEE OF "STUPID PET TRICKS" BECOMES A PUBLICITY HOUND

It was as startling as a wedge of apple pie on a tray full of sushi. There, in the middle of Manhattan's swank Electron discotheque and rock club, The Ritz, were all the old familiar faces — Billy ("An Innocent Man") Joel with his "Uptown Girl" megahypersupermodel Christie Brinkley; Brooke ("Bob Hope Special") Shields and ultramegasuperstar Michael Jackson; Cornelia ("Nothing") Guest and Andy Warhol; Susan Saint ("Kate and Allie") James and her unidentified husband — when Jacqueline ("A Tour of the White House") Onassis paid a surprise visit. The incredible

O commanded all eyes, then broke into a charming smile that revealed a carefully blacked-out space between her two front teeth. "I'm just here to see David," whispered the former First Lady.

Get in line, Jackie. David ("Late Night with David Letterman") Letterman was finishing a fast dance with cover girls Sharon (*Vogue*) Hill and Terri (*Sports Illustrated* "Swimsuit Edition") Malone, after which he quickly stopped by Mike Nichols's table, presumably to discuss his forthcoming one-man Broadway show, "My Oh My! It's David Letterman!" Then the clown prince of late-night TV slipped out a side door, eluding Jackie and roaring off in his specially designed double-decker limousine/hydrofoil.

Neither rain nor snow nor gloom of night stops *this* Letterman from making the rounds...of parties. How does this fit in with the folksy Letterman image, which is more Winnebago than Rolls Royce? "Look," said David through a mouthful of caviar, "the David Letterman you see on TV is a *character*. That's acting. That isn't me, any more than Leonard Nimoy is the Vulcan Spock. On TV, my 'David Letterman' character is this gee-shucks Midwestern guy, right? Well, the *real* Dave Letterman happens to be a very talented and intelligent individual who just happens to be a star in this very difficult industry we call the entertainment industry." He wraps up the remaining caviar in a thousand-dollar bill and shoves it in his pocket, leaves the waitress a Late-Night Facial Blotter in lieu of a tip, and strolls off to the NBC studio where he will once again become "David Letterman."

photo by Christopher Little

9:47 p.m. David pulls up in front of New York's Ritz rock club, and exits his car as flashbulbs pop.

photo by Christopher Little

9:59 p.m. "Now I'm really having more fun than humans should be allowed," chortles Dave, with his Boilermaker (J.D. and Bud) at his elbow, as he scans the club for what he calls "new talent."

10:08 p.m. "Being a talk-show host is great practice for talking to girls," points out David, here with a new found friend. He seems to have mastered the art.

10:21 p.m. "I live to boogy!" says David, as he shakes a leg under the giant video screens, here with another new found friend.

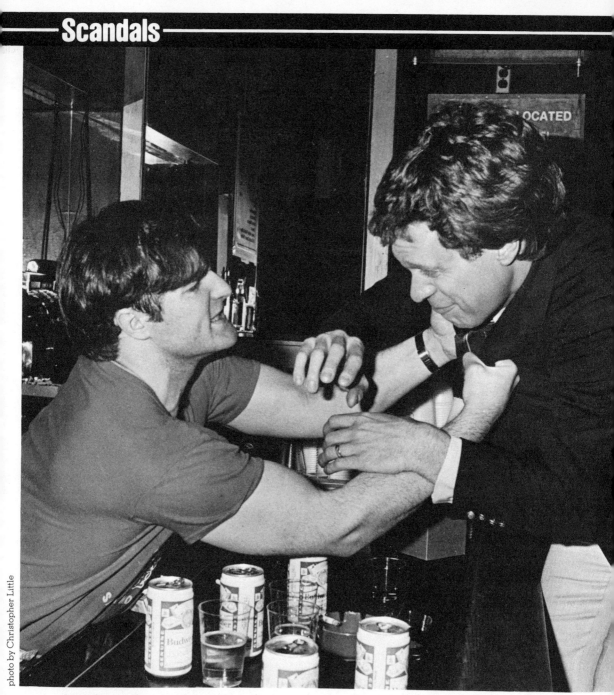

photo by Christopher Little

10:34 p.m. Dave returns to the bar for another boilermaker, but... "You've had enough, pal," growls the friendly bartender. "You're starting to get obnoxious." "But you don't understand," protests David, "I'm like this all the time."

10:40 p.m. Dave is escorted out, personally, by the club's personnel. "Are you guys trying to tell me something?" quips David. "I've been thrown out of better places than *this*."

10:45 p.m. All in all, a successful night on the town. David leaves, tired but happy, until tomorrow night once again brings out the party-animal called David Letterman.

Sunday Ledger

PARADE

LAUGHING IT UP WITH ED McMAHON

By Joe Piscopo

Catherine Calder from TV's "Dunwood Heights" Explains Who She Is and What Her Show Is About, and It Still Doesn't Ring a Bell

The War In Central America

SIDEKICKS, FALL GUYS, AND SECOND BANANAS TAKE HEART!

ED MCMAHON ALWAYS KEEPS HIS SPIRITS UP

*T*onto never broke out of it. Neither did Kato, Dr. Watson, or David Nelson — they were always the second banana. However, Ed McMahon, once thought to be little more than Johnny Carson's laugh-track, is breaking out of the sidekick role with a vengeance. He is now not only the star of one network show ("TV's Bloopers and Practical Jokes") and one highly successful syndicated show ("Ed McMahon's Star Search"), but he also pops up in commercials for publishers' sweepstakes, vague insurance companies and the ubiquitous Budweiser promotions. PARADE sent Joe to talk to the former second banana now tops in the bunch.

Joe: *Let's talk about Ed McMahon. Why are you always laughing?*

Ed: Ha ha ha ha ha ha ha ha ha ha! I'm a jolly guy, Joe.

Joe: *Yes, you are.*

Ed: Ha ha ha ha ha ha ha! Good one, Joe!

Joe: *Let me just try something here. Ed, your house has been demolished.*

Ed: Ha ha ha ha ha ha ha ha!

Joe: *As a matter of fact, the whole town was destroyed in a freak nuclear accident.*

Ed: Ha ha ha ha ha ha ha ha!

Joe: *And the brewery blew up.*

Ed: What?!

Joe: *Just kidding, Ed.*

Ed: That's not funny, Joe. You don't fool around with a guy's Clydesdales.

Joe: *I'm sorry. Let's talk about "Star Search."*

Ed: Ha ha ha ha ha ha ha ha! Let's.

Joe: *I love "Star Search." It's a big hit, too. Do you have any interest in expanding the show?*

Ed: Ha ha ha ha ha ha! Yes. I've discovered that many, many people want new stars to get found. But many, many, MANY people also want some of our *old* stars to get *lost.*

Joe: *Really?*

Ed: Ha ha ha. That's why my next show will be called "Star Dump." Two well-known stars will compete—for example, Charlene Tilton and Sally Struthers might go head-to-head in the Leading Lady category. Then our judges vote between them. Whoever loses is dumped in the ocean and lost forever! Ha ha ha ha ha ha!

Joe: *Wouldn't there be inherent problems in that?*

Ed: Only if we're followed by "Sea Hunt," and Lloyd Bridges rediscovers them! Ha ha ha ha ha ha ha ha!

Joe: *Did you think of the "spokesmodel" category on "Star Search"?*

Ed: Ha ha ha ha ha ha ha! No. When I first heard the term "spokesmodel," I thought it was a woman who wore a bicycle wheel around her neck! Get it? "Spokes" model! Ha ha ha ha ha ha!

Joe: *Good one, Ed.*

Ed: Ha ha ha ha ha ha ha ha ha! Want a blast of this?

Joe: *Not this early in the morning, thanks.*

Ed: What's the matter? Do you need a glass? Never use one myself! Ha ha ha ha ha!

Joe: *No thanks, I'm really not thirsty. But enough about "Star Search." Let's go on.*

Ed: Ha ha ha ha! Good idea. It's amazing, but on that little reel of tape there, you've already asked me *every possible question* about "Star Search"! As a matter of fact, you've managed, in a few minutes, to ask me every single *imaginable* question in the world that could possibly ever be asked *ever,* about "Star Search"! Every single question, right there on that tiny little reel of tape! It's unbelievable! You've covered it entirely, every conceivable angle on "Star Search"!

Joe: *Wrong, casting-couch-breath.*

Ed: Ha ha ha ha ha ha ha ha ha ha ha ha ha!

Joe: *But forget it. Let's go on to your other show: "TV's Bloopers and Practical Jokes."*

Ed: Ha ha ha ha ha ha. I laugh just thinking about it, Joe.

Joe: *First, explain what a blooper is.*

Ed: A blooper is something on TV that is completely unplanned, silly or obscene, and it reveals someone screwing up.

Joe: *Oh, like a presidential press conference.*

Ed: Ha ha ha ha ha ha ha ha! No, John, a blooper isn't like that!

Joe: *My name is Joe.*

Ed: Whoops! ! *I* did a blooper! Say, I'll use that one on my next show! We're starting to run a little low, I'm afraid. Pretty soon we'll have to start taping them ourselves.

Joe: *The programs are certainly popular. Every network now has a "blooper" show.*

Ed: Ha ha ha ha ha! Yes, ABC and CBS have blooper shows, too. But ours is always the best. When it comes to screwing up, nobody beats NBC!

Joe: *I'll say.*

Ed: Ha ha ha ha ha ha ha ha ha ha!

Joe: *How about the "Practical Jokes" segment of the show?*

Ed: That's where we play tricks on people, just to see the wacky looks on their faces! Its very funny! Ha ha ha ha ha!

Joe: *Could you give us some examples?*

Ed: Sure! Dick Clark and I called up Sammy Davis, Jr., who is a very close, very dear friend of both of ours. We asked him if he had Prince Albert in a can. And he said—ha ha ha ha ha ha ha ha!—he said, "No. You must be trying to call a tobacco store. This is a private home." Ha ha ha ha ha ha! Sammy is quite a good sport! You should have

seen his face! It was a classic television moment.

Joe: *Are any of the jokes more elaborate?*

Ed: Ha ha ha ha ha ha! Sure! Some of them take a lot of planning! For example, a few years ago, we were doing our first "Blooper" show as a special. We went up to Washington state, to a little town in the mountains. And we wondered just what would happen if one of those mountains suddenly just *blew up*! Ha ha ha ha ha ha ha! How would people react?

Joe: *Mount Saint Helens?*

Ed: You saw the show!

Joe: *You did that?*

Ed: Ha ha ha ha ha ha! It was a lot of planning, for both Dick and myself. But it was all worth it when we saw the looks on people's faces! Were they surprised! Ha ha ha ha ha ha ha ha!

Joe: *Well, we've talked about "Star Search" and "TV's Bloopers and Practical Jokes." What about your other television work?*

Ed: Ha ha. What other television work?

Joe: *"The Tonight Show."*

Ed: Ha ha ha ha ha ha ha ha ha ha ha ha! Well, 1 don't really consider that work. I just sit there and do this: Ha ha ha ha ha ha ha ha ha ha ha ha!

Joe: *"Ha ha ha ha ha ha ha ha ha ha ha ha ha"?*

Ed: Hey, you're good! Ha ha ha HA HA ha ha ha!

Joe: *Ha ha ha HA HA ha ha ha!*

Ed: Try this one: HHO-ohh!

Joe: *HHO-ohh!*

Ed: You've got a big future, kid.

Joe: *Ha ha ha!*

Special Feature: Is the Counterculture Dead?

RollingStone

FRANK SINATRA
Ol' Blue Eyes is Blasting the Rock Scene

Lauren Tewes Talks About Life After "The Love Boat"

Crabgrass

Rating the Personal Computer

Perfectly Frank

──── The Rolling Stone Interview ────

Inside the Penthouse Suite at Atlantic City's Golden Nugget Hotel, businessmen move in and out, paying their respects. Bouquets of flowers bearing notes of appreciation from senators, congressmen and other entertainers fill the room.

In the midst of all the activity, the man sat, quietly sipping tea, resting his golden voice for tonight's sold-out, SRO concert for over 500 of the Golden Nugget's preferred customers. His famous blue eyes swept across the room. Downstairs, a limo was waiting to take him to Ellington Air Force Base after the concert. *Air Force One* stood by waiting to fly him to Geneva, where he promised to "do what he could" at the arms limitations talks.

It was just another day in the life of Francis Albert Sinatra.

ROLLING STONE: It's a pleasure to meet you.

SINATRA: Likewise. Speak.

ROLLING STONE: First of all, your political connections.

SINATRA: One moment, my friend. I thought this was a music magazine.

ROLLING STONE: We also cover politics.

SINATRA: Marvelous. Record reviews *and* international affairs. Stick to the rock-and-roll, baby, it's what you do best and you're struggling at that.

ROLLING STONE: How about off the record? Just one question . . . you've had close ties with heads of state, royalty, and world leaders . . .

Suddenly a dark-suited mesomorph beckoned me to the door with a single finger that bespoke authority.

ROLLING STONE: Just one more question . . .

SINATRA: Ciao baby.

There were to be no more questions, no more answers. The Chairman of the Board had spoken.

photo by Troy Miller

"Some innocent times."

55

"Some cuchoo times."

"Some very good years."

LIFE

AMERICA'S SCENIC ACCESS RAMPS

ONE DAY IN THE LIFE OF A DRY CLEANER

JOE PISCOPO, THE SPORTS GUY,

TALKS ABOUT SPORTS: THE AMERICAN OBSESSION

Talking with "The Sports Guy"

Here's "The Sports Guy" with "Cassius Clay" way back when.

When Joe Piscopo starts to talk about sports, it's almost as though he becomes another person. In fact, he *does* become another person —a second personality that identifies itself only as "The Sports Guy." Some might say that carrying sports-mania to the point of outright schizophrenia may be going a bit far, but nevertheless, "The Sports Guy's" neat summaries of the sports scene are irresistible.

Who *is* "The Sports Guy"? Take Howard himself, Marv Albert, Warner Wolf, Keith Jackson, not to mention a dozen small-market sports announcers, then you might begin to understand him. Not many people get to see the private life of this intense individual. *Life* recently spent a day with "The Sports Guy" chatting, among other things, about the one thing this guy lives for: Sports!

We began the day in his luxury box overlooking the fifty-yard line of Giants Stadium in Rutherford, New Jersey.

photo courtesy of NBC

Here they are twenty years later.

LIFE: This is a beautiful box.

SG: THANKS!

LIFE: How much time do you spend here?

SG: PARDON?

LIFE: Being a sports reporter, you must spend a lot of time in a place like this, but you don't live here, do you?...heh-heh...

SG: YES!

LIFE: Pardon?

SG: YES!

LIFE: You live in a luxury box at Giants Stadium?

SG: CORRECT!

LIFE: Which explains the welcome mat at the stadium entrance. Why would you want to live *here*?

SG: MEADOWLANDS! COMPLEX! AWESOME! ARENA: HOCKEY! BASKETBALL! STADIUM: FOOTBALL! SOCCER! ALSO: RACING! HORSES!

LIFE: And we understand that there will soon be a baseball team coming to the New Jersey Meadowlands. Are they thinking of a name?

SG: THE CHEMICALS!

LIFE: Could you describe, in your own word(s), a day in the life of "The Sports Guy"?

SG: MORNING. UP. JOG. SHOWERS. BREAKFAST. VENDORS. HOT DOGS. BEER. DRIVE. WORK. LIMO? HAH! NETWORK. CHEAP! OFFICE. NEW YORK. ATHLETES...STADIUMS...INTERVIEWS...LUNCH. 21? SHEA! WORK. AGAIN. EXCITING...THRILLING...BORING... HOME! BED. NOOKIE. SLEEP."

LIFE: What do you do for recreation?

SG: CONCERTS!

LIFE: At the arena?

SG: ABSOLUTELY!

LIFE: Who are among your favorite performers?

SG: FRANK! BRUCE! JERRY!

"The Sports Guy" explaining the NFL/Baseball playoffs. As he said at the time, "WHO WINS? WHO KNOWS? WHO CARES?!?"

LIFE: Lewis?

SG: VALE!

LIFE: Jerry Vale?

SG: ANTHEM. AWESOME!

LIFE: We seem to be getting the hang of this. Uh...word association?

SG: SURE!

LIFE: Baseball.

SG: JAIL!

LIFE: Tennis?

SG: PING-PONG!

LIFE: Phil Rizzuto.

SG: COOPERSTOWN!

LIFE: Steve Carlton.

SG:

LIFE: NCAA.

SG: NBA!

LIFE: NHL.

SG: WBC!

LIFE: LPGA.

SG: T N' A!

LIFE: USFL.

SG: ABC-TVFL!

LIFE: NFL.

SG: C-O-K-E!

LIFE: That was fun!

SG: HYSTERICAL.

LIFE: Before we end our little interview, our readers would love to see what you think of yourself. How would *you* describe "The Sports Guy"?

SG: MALE! 32! 6'1". 170 LBS. EYES. HAZEL! HAIR. BROWN!

Here are some of "The Sports Guy's" more memorable moments on television.

"The Sports Guy" giving The Champ advice on boxing.

photo by Mark Mullen

"The Sports Guy" giv Herschel Walker advi on necks.

NFL? MLB? NBA? YES!

"The Sports Guy" giving advice to Don King on fashion.

GQ

WHINERSTYLE
Doug Whiner's Looks For Work And Play Speak For Themselves

THE MANLY ART OF SHOPPING

MEN AND THEIR MANLY FRIENDSHIPS

MALE MASCULINITY AND THE MANLY GENTLEMAN

WHY MANLINESS IS BACK IN STYLE

AND A POEM BY GERARD MANLEY HOPKINS

by Christopher Little

WHINER

The High-pitched High-style of Doug Whiner

STYLE:

Throughout the vagaries of fashion, it is Style that endures. Some men have it, or It, perhaps—a natural, artless ordering of the wardrobe. As natural and artless as the order of their lives. The man with style is a man who doesn't think about his clothes. They think about *him*. Or seem to, when huddling together on their hangers in the dark recesses of his closet.

The man with style. Ideally, he is indistinguishable from the clothes he wears. Indeed, if the man is truly stylish, he is *so* indistinguishable from the clothes he wears that he can lay one of his suits on a chair and his children will ask it questions; his boss will promote it; and his best friend's wife will make a pass at it. She's always been a bit of a tippler, so perhaps that doesn't count. But nonetheless, it's the power of Style.

The man with style. His clothes are an easy counterpart to his life, just like his friends. And like his friends, some of his clothes are rough-woven or are of strange and frightening colors or have ridiculously wide lapels. But, just like his friends, he can always have his clothes altered, because his clothes *are* his friends. And, as with friends, he feels perfectly comfortable sitting around with his clothes having a little chat with them, or perhaps throwing a little tea party to honor them. Such is the man with style.

The man with style, as we have said, rejects fashion. Hence, the style of Douglas Whiner.

Douglas, or "Doug," as intimates call him, is an American original. If Oscar Wilde was on the mark when he said that discontent is the first step in the progress of a man or a nation, then Whiner has progressed further than any man in our memory. Always alive to the creature comforts—and particularly to their absence—Whiner looks for clothes that feel good as well as look good. "Ohhhhh," he explains. "I *hate* clothes that hurrrrt. Like right now! These pants *itchhhh!* This underwear is tooooo tight! Everything's all wronnnnng!" The attention to detail is a Whinerstyle trademark.

Another unmistakable sign of Whinerstyle is Doug's insistence on easy-care clothes—undoubtably the influence of his charming mate, Wendy Whiner, who also spoke to us. "Ohhhhhhh," drones the winsome Wendy, "I have to do *every*thing! I do all the *ironing!* I do all the *washing!* I do all the *mending!* I do all the *shopping!* I have to do everyyything! All Doug does is weeeaaaaarrrr the clothes!"

And wear them well indeed. Here, then, is Doug Whiner, whose voice speaks clearly through his clothes.

photo by Christopher Little

Whinerstyle is always a manstyle, and nowhere is this more evident than in the masculine reaches of the outdoors. Pioneer Doug loves the wide-open spaces, except for the bugs, the dirt, the snakes, the weather and the fact that there's no place to sit down when you're outdoors, except on some rotten log that's covered with dirty bark or else some rock that has scorpions and lizards under it, probably. Doug wears a classic plaid shirt ($60) and jeans by Evan ($75). His ax is from Rite-Value Hardware ($30) and is way too heavy, according to Lumberjack Doug.

Our Wall Street analyst predicts a bull market for this conservative young man's suit, by Dillon ($650). "Six hundred and fifty dollars for a suit?" groans Whiner. "Whyyyyyyyyyyyyy? Huhhhhhhhhhh?" His leather attaché is from Doone and Hill ($275) but the clasps don't work very well, Doug informs us. The horn-rimmed glasses ($200) are from Mario Opticals. "But I don't neeeeeeed glasses!" Doug protests charmingly to our fashion editor. "You'll wear them and like them," our frustrated editor replies. "But it's all blurrrrrry. I can't read this newspaper! And where's the sports section?" persists Doug.

photo by Christopher Little

Horseracing may be the sport of kings, but polo remains the sport of princes—including England's Prince Charles and our own Prince Whining, Doug. The polo pants are from Russell Allen ($125) and are simultaneously too tight and too loose, according to Doug, who also commented that he was tired, modeling was boring and our photographer's lights were too hot. "I'm afraid of horses," claims Doug, "and they smell terrrrrrible! What am I supposed to do with this croquet mallet? This helmet is squashing my ears! I'm getting a headache!" We gave him some Excedrin ($2.99) and took a few ourselves.

photo by Christopher Little

"Land ho!" says Captain Doug. "It's probably an iceberg. We're going to sink, hellllp!" He's sporting white flannel trousers ($150), navy silk and wool jacket ($375), and a nattily knotted silk scarf ("Sillllk!? Eeeeuuuww! That comes from worrrrrrrms! And this scarf is choking me to death! Hellllp, I'm getting seasick! Look, there's a sharrrrrk!" adds Doug.) Anchors aweigh!

photo by Christopher Little

A seemingly endless high-pitched note, capable of shattering glass—the trained voice of a world-famous soprano. "Big deal," whines Doug, our operagoer. "My wife, Wendy, can do the same thing when she's calling me in from the garage." Doug's tuxedo is from Patrick's Formal Wear ($20 a day, $100 deposit) and his matching tie and cummerbund set it off to perfection. "This cummerbund is awwwwwful," says Whiner. "I can't wear this! I've got diverticulitis!" It's high style in the days of Whiner and roses.

photo by Christopher Little

CELEBRITY HAIRSTYLES

NEWSMAN TED KOPPEL

IS INDUCTED INTO HAIRSTYLING'S HALL-OF-FAME

THE THREE LOOKS FOR THIS SEASON:
SHORT, MEDIUM, AND LONG

THE PERILS OF HOME PERMANENTS,
BY MTV'S NINA BLACKWOOD

DURABLE HAIRSPRAYS:
ONE SPRITZ HOLDS YOUR 'DO
FOR FIVE TO SIX YEARS.

LATHER, RINSE, REPEAT...

HOW TO KNOW WHEN TO
BREAK THE VICIOUS CYCLE

Hair Styling Hall-of-Famer TED KOPPEL

"The active career man has to find
a 'do with wash 'n' wear ease
as well as casual sophistication,"
sez Ted Koppel, this month's
Hair Styling Hall-of-Fame inductee.
"My coif is super for work and play,
and every season of the year."

HAIR STYLING: How did you hit upon this particular look?

KOPPEL: I really can't take the credit. It was my stylist, Mr. Bob, who figured it out. If I may speak frankly, I had been under the impression that my fine, limp hair lacked the body to hold a set like this. And with my busy schedule and late nights, I simply didn't have the time to spend hours fussing with it. Now I just get the layer cut every week or so, condition it daily, then damp set with styling gel or mousse on giant rollers. When dry, it brushes out easily into this flattering, side-parted confection.

HAIR STYLING: The color is really beautiful. I don't know why people are always comparing it to Howdy Doody or Alfred E. Neuman's hair.

KOPPEL: I'm used to it. I think it's because there are no other red-headed newsmen. All the national newspeople are brunette if they're men, blonde if they're women. Red hair is not associated with authoritative reporting. It's associated with Lucille Ball, Bozo, and the aforementioned Howdy Doody, and Alfred E. Neuman —all fine entertainment figures, but hardly models of credibility on any level.

HAIR STYLING: Does it bother you that all this attention goes to your hair?

KOPPEL: At first, I fought it. I thought it was rather silly that it was a topic at all, and preferred to discuss only news and journalism. I suppose I wanted people to ignore the fact that there was forty pounds of bright red hair sitting on top of my head—an unrealistic proposal, at best.

HAIR STYLING: Your style is similar to the one Princess Di wore at the royal wedding, when she took the hairdo world by storm.

KOPPEL: Yes, but she's wearing it a bit longer now. I saw the ABC news footage, and it's definitely longer. My cut is closer to Melissa Manchester's, as of the moment, as you will see if you check your sources.

HAIR STYLING: So you do think hair styling is as important as the news you cover?

KOPPEL: Sometimes, it's even more important. Look at all the discussion that was held regarding President Reagan's hair. Everyone wanted to know if he dyed it, and why he wore it in a style usually seen on in-bred gas-station attendants in rural areas. When I moderated the first Democratic debate in 1984, Alan Cranston was asked if he, too, was dying his hair. People care about it. If people care about it, it's news.

HAIR STYLING: Do you think hair makes a difference in people's perceptions of other public figures?

KOPPEL: I believe that is indisputable. Imagine Indira Gandhi with Margaret Thatcher's hair. They are two completely different prime ministers. Indira wears a no-fuss, no-frills sleek chignon, and her lustrous black hair is accentuated with that special silver streak that is hers alone. Margaret opts for a formal look, with carefully arranged waves ending in a flip. She uses a great deal of hairspray, giving the impression that she could fall down and break her hair if she doesn't take care. And perhaps you can recall a few years ago, when her image counselor told her to dye her hair a darker blonde. That was considered newsworthy and and duly reported by all the media, including my own network. We cannot hold public figures to standards that we ourselves are unwilling to abide by, hence, I must be willing to discuss *my* hair as honestly as I discuss Thatcher's.

HAIR STYLING: Terrific! Tell us. Do you have any secret peeves about your coif?

KOPPEL: It's practical and *sportif*, but it's not very versatile, to be absolutely candid. The styling options are rather limited.

HAIR STYLING: We can help you there! Just put yourself into our hands and *you'll* be making headlines yourself!

photo by Mark Mullen/Bob Pook

Here is Ted's everyday look, perfect for the office or for covering the daily beat. We brushed it with a flat, natural-bristle brush for maximum volume and lift, then smoothed it back to highlight Ted's classic features.

This look is carefree, curly and casual,
suitable for a summer conference at Camp David
or any time Ted feels like a softer, tousled look.
A few ringlets escape for the windblown effect.

Same man, same hair, but the look says Now! This very contemporary style takes some doing, but its dramatic statement is worth it. Ted says he will wear this young, hip coif in London next spring for the unemployment riots.

Dinner at the White House? This elegant evening look will take you there, then on the air, without a hitch. Ted's delivery will be as smooth as this upsweep, just this side of sultry, but still every inch a gentleman. Turn ends under with a curling iron for a demure look. No matter how he wears his hair, Ted's style and charisma carry the day.

AMERICAN
WRENCH & SCREWDRIVER

JOHNNY
"MR. SCREWDRIVER"
BELSON
TALKS ABOUT
THE NEW
1985 DRIVERS

DON'T MONKEY AROUND
WITH YOUR
MONKEY WRENCH

DRIVEABLE HANDLES:
HANDLE WITH CARE!

WRENCH OR
SCREWDRIVER?
CHOOSE-THE-RIGHT-TOOL
QUIZ

AND
AN INTERVIEW WITH
JOE PISCOPPO

American Wrench & Screwdriver

gets a drop-forged, chrome vanadium interview with

JOE PISCOPPO

WE SENT OUR ACE SOCKET-WRENCH EDITOR, DALE DORRETT, ON A SPECIAL INTERVIEW THIS MONTH. HIS REGULAR COLUMN "SOCKET TO ME" WILL RESUME NEXT ISSUE.

photo by Christopher Little

AMERICAN WRENCH AND SCREWDRIVER: *Hello there, Joe Piscopo.*

JOE: *Hi, Dale.*

AWAS: *So!*

JOE: *So.*

AWAS: *What exactly is it that you do again?*

JOE: *I'm primarily an actor, but I'm doing interviews to promote my new book.*

AWAS: *Oh. I'm the socket-wrench editor at* American Wrench and Screwdriver.
(there is some silence)

AWAS: *What kind of things do you act?*

JOE: *I guess I'm best known for my television work, on a . . .*

AWAS: *Oh! Television! Sure! I have a TV myself! Great model, chassis model 12YB3X, 120 volts, 60Hz, 0.4 AMPS.*

JOE: *Did you ever see my HBO special?*

AWAS: *No. I'll tell you the truth, Joe. The only programs that are any good are the ones that come on Sundays around 2:00 P.M., that is, when they're not pre-empted by some stupid sporting event. That's about the only time you can find any programming at all about tool care and workshop safety.*

JOE: *So you don't know very much about TV, huh?*

AWAS: *Well, I never watch the damn thing. I fix it a lot, though. A socket wrench is no good at all on a job like that, of course. I use an ordinary Phillips screwdriver to open the back, and inside, on the more delicate parts, I find neither a wrench nor a screwdriver is a propos! Needle-nose pliers are the ticket, once you're inside. Of course, most sets do have a warning on the back saying, "No user-serviceable parts inside" and they discourage tinkering, but the home craftsman is more capable than they think — that is, with a little elbow grease and a pair of needle-nose pliers! But we're way off the subject now. This magazine is not about needle-nose pliers…it's about wrenches! And screwdrivers! So tell us about your book!*

JOE: *Well, I've just completed the book which is entitled,* The Piscopo Tapes. *It's basically a compilation of celebrity interviews, and I'm very excited about it.*

AWAS: *How is a book like that put together?*

JOE: *We started with a basic idea, or "concept" if you will, and then chose the topics to be covered. Then we tried to think of humorous "takes" on those topics.*

AWAS: *No, I meant how is it put together? No screws or bolts, I guess?*

JOE: *No, I don't think so. I'm not really sure. Could it be glued?*

AWAS: *Paper and similarly porous materials can, of course, be glued; however, the use of glue can sometimes lead to a sticky mess! The average craftsman is better off using more solid materials, even in an amateur "Weekend Workshop." I don't know if this applies to books per se, though.*

JOE: *I don't either.*

AWAS: *Hmmm. Interesting. So tell me more about this book. It's a joke book?*

JOE: *It takes a humorous point of view, yes. We try to laugh at the little flaws and foibles that plague us all as we stumble through the human comedy.*

AWAS: *Do you have any yarns or anecdotes that we could use in "Gut-Wrenchers"? That's our monthly humor column.*

JOE: *There are a lot of stories I could tell you! (laughs) Okay, here's one. Jerry Lewis and Eddie Murphy were both getting ready to . . .*

AWAS: *Excuse me. Does this have anything to do with wrenches or screwdrivers, at all? I forgot, that's one of the things it has to be.*

JOE: *Not really. There's a shovel in it, how about that?*

AWAS: *Well. Gee. Go on, anyway.*

JOE: *I have a feeling you don't really want to hear this.*

AWAS: *No, no . . . no, I don't, Joe. But go ahead and finish it, and then we'll get back on the subject.*

JOE: *So, anyway, it seems that they were both trying to get into the* same . . . and neither of them . . . uh, I forget. It had something to do with the television show. Never mind.

AWAS: *What was the name of that show again?*

JOE: *"The Joe Piscopo Special" — it was a one-hour comedy special that . . .*

AWAS: *You know something you ought to spoof guys who always use the wrong tool! (See related article: "Choose the Right Tool!", p.58). Everybody knows some guy who never fails to fit a wrench imperfectly, and ends up rounding off the corners of the bolt.*

JOE: *They'll do it every time!*

AWAS: *Or you could do a guy who is trying to get some screws out in a hurry. Only the thing is, he uses too much force on a soft metal and he ends up breaking the slots on all the screws! Then he has to kiss the whole project good-bye! Did you ever think of doing something like that, on that show?*

JOE: *Well, it's really more of a feature film idea.*

AWAS: *Well, you're welcome to use it, you don't have to pay me or anything, if that's what's holding you back. Okay, here's another one. A take-off on the film* Taxi Driver, *called* Screw Driver. *A Vietnam vet, who used to be in the Army Corps of Engineers, comes home and gets a boring job in a fix-it shop. All day he's surrounded by broken, greasy engines, and he finally just gets fed up, shaves his hair into a Mohawk, goes crazy . . .*

JOE: *You mean, he "gets a screw loose"?*

AWAS: *Hey! That's great! I guess*

that's why you're a professional and I'm not. I wouldn't have thought of that. Of course, you wouldn't have thought of the Dorrett Lug Wrench. That's what makes the world go round and round.

JOE: *The Dorrett Lug Wrench?*

AWAS: *No, the difference between one guy and another. The Dorrett Lug Wrench is my own design, a variation on the standard that's pretty revolutionary. Well, this has been a very interesting talk, Mr. Piscopo.*

JOE: *It has?*

AWAS: *Not really, but thanks for coming by.*

JOE: *My pleasure.*

EPILOGUE:

The Making of *The Piscopo Tapes*

The making of any book is a collaborative effort, from the lumberjacks who cut down the trees for the paper to the guys who get the ink from wherever the hell ink comes from. We would be remiss if we were not to mention each one of these people by name, and believe me, we'd like to, because the publisher has requested 10,000 more words and has started bandying about terms like *contract* and *sue* — legal jargon that is supposed to frighten the artistes, and certainly does the job. If there were only 5,000 people we could acknowledge, and they both had two names, we would be on Easy Street, and could take that cruise to the Cayman Islands we've been postponing. If we could get these fellows' *middle* names, as well, we would need even fewer people to thank; that is, ten thousand divided by three. You figure it out. We are too tired.

You see, it's not such an easy thing writing a book. One must choose one's words carefully, and then one must get them in the proper order. Sometimes this

photo by Christopher Little

"Graphic artist, Bob Pook, took precious time from his hectic schedule at "Saturday Night Live" and "Late Night with David Letterman" to perform some of his magic here."

87

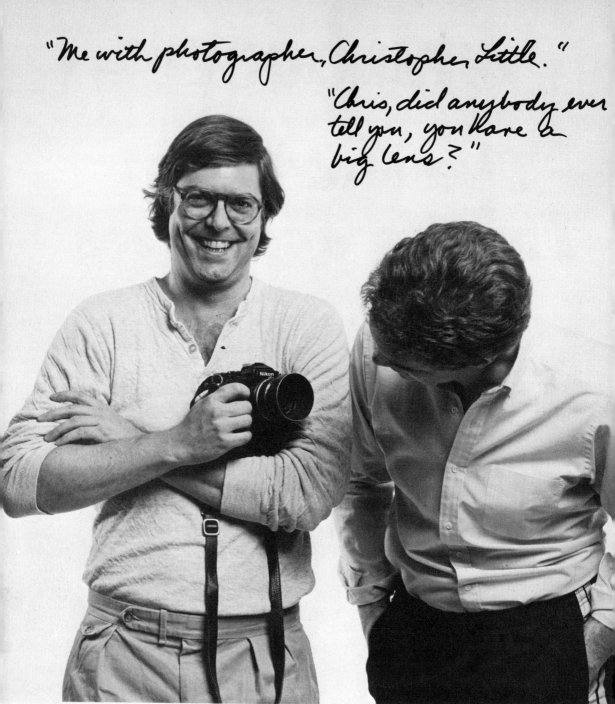

"Me with photographer, Christopher Little."

"Chris, did anybody ever tell you, you have a big lens?"

photo by Christopher Little

takes a great deal of time. Sometimes one even needs to go on a cruise to the Cayman Islands to relax, before starting work. Okay, I *already* took the cruise — me being Pam, who is at the typewriter right now. Well, *I* didn't take any cruise when we were *supposed* to be working (this is Joe typing now). Yeah, well, you

went off to Malibu, as I recall. Well, that was business. (Here you see illustrated another bugaboo of this book-collaboration business. You have two voices speaking in one book, and aside from using pink and blue ink alternately, there's no way to tell who's writing at the moment. Some people claim that they can "hear" the voice on the printed page and can tell the difference. You should be careful where you claim something like this, because if you can "hear" a book talking to you, it may not be long until your kitchen appliances and your laundry may be "talking" to you as well, which means you will get a one-way trip to the Acorn Academy for a "rest.") Granted, we did both take vacations in February, when this book was originally due. Pam took the now-famous cruise to the Caymans, in order to research humor patterns in the cheap gag-books of the ancient Incas, a venture that became suspect when it was discovered that the Incas did not live anywhere near the Cayman Islands (and were probably unaware of the tax advantages therein) and furthermore, that the Incas were not involved in the gift-book industry at all, instead choosing to amuse themselves by building ziggurats or something. Joe went to California and sat on the beach, which was very calming and relaxing, a state of mind which is utterly unhelpful to the unpleasant and frenzied busines of joke-writing. The proper state of mind for this sort of undertaking is one similar to "My Friend Flicka's" when she was being led out of the burning barn. So that pretty much shot February.

In March, we were both very upset about the breakup of AT&T. This apparently happened some time ago, but we didn't hear about it until March, okay? Anyway, a lot of designated "writing time" was taken up, trying to figure out what was going on. As best as we can figure, AT&T was broken down into a lot of smaller companies that will give us lousy

service at higher prices, and the public is allegedly glad about it, because AT&T won't be making as much money. This is supposed to give us some kind of malicious pleasure, that we would gladly pay higher phone bills to attain. The whole thing sounds kind of petty to us. *Then,* AT&T hires Cliff Robertson to do their com-

"Me with Annette Bianco, my wig mistress. That's my own hair, here."

mercials, a transparent ploy if ever there was one. This fellow is supposed to have a lot of credibility because (a) he's got that rich wife so everyone figures he's not doing it for the money, but out of sheer passion for the American Telephone and Telegraph Company; and (b) he blew the whistle on some Hollywood mogul who gave him a $10,000 rubber check. (That (b) is a credential for sainthood is particularly perplexing. In our part of the country, quaintly enough, checks are taken seriously as a medium of exchange. What do people in Hollywood *usually* do when they get a bad check for ten grand? Dismiss it with an airy laugh? It's possible, I suppose, and it would actually explain a lot of things, like why movies about dancing teenagers are coming in at forty or fifty million dollars. It's all those overdrafts.) So that took care of March.

Then it was April, and we had the whole thing just about ready to type up (really, it was all in our heads, it was just a question of putting it into words), but there was the little matter of filling out income tax forms. (For people from the Cayman Islands, who don't pay any taxes, we will explain: Annoyingly enough, our government not only makes

photo by Christopher

"Me with Mark Klein my wardrobe master. these are my own clothes, here."

photo by Christopher Little

"Me with Kevin Haney, my make up genius. That's my own face, here. I think."

everybody give them a big box of money every year, but it makes us *figure out the bill ourselves,* which is tantamount to making the condemned man rig up his own electric chair with a coat hanger and an old flashlight battery. You don't want to do it wrong, but you don't particularly want to do it right, either.) But although we didn't get any work done on the book in April, one of us did manage to deduct the unfinished manuscript from all taxes by declaring it as an oil well. Apparently, that's the subtitle of this book: *The Piscopo Tapes: An Oil Well.* I'm not saying which one of us it was, but it's the one of us with a deep, masculine voice.

So April passed (that sounds very beautiful. I think we're getting the hang of this literary stuff after all) and Simon and Schuster started getting testy. I guess Simon and Schuster *never* had problems getting a project going! Oh no, not them! They're PER-FECT!! (This, coincidentally, is a good illustration of another problem in bookwriting: sarcasm. It doesn't come across in print. Go back and read those last few sentences, but imagine us being really sarcastic and rolling our eyes. Changes the meaning, doesn't it?)

91

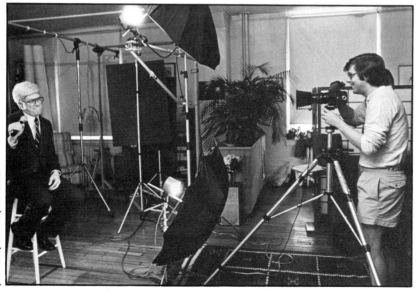

93

photo by Christopher Little

"Pam with her travel agent (see page 88)."

Is this ten thousand words yet?

If we were still in college, we would pull one of those clever term-paper tricks at this point, such as the inclusion of a long quotation to fill up space. But as a wise man (a professor of ours) once said, "The use of a long and ofttimes inappropriate quotation in the context of an essay in order to fill up space, fools no one and only makes a fool of the one who employs this silly subterfuge, since brevity is the soul of good writing, as Abraham Lincoln so aptly illustrated in the pithy-but-immortal address which every schoolchild knows: 'Fourscore and seven years ago, our fathers brought forth on this continent a new nation, conceived in liberty and dedicated to the proposition that all men are created equal. Now we are engaged in a great civil war, testing whether this nation, or any nation so conceived and so dedicated, can long endure. We are met on a great battlefield of that war.' It goes on from here, and it's a real humdinger of a speech — at least, it used to really knock out audiences in the days before politicians decided to start saying

by Christopher Little

"Me and Pam with editor, Melissa Newman, the two women who occupy my life."

'Where's the beef?' to get a laugh, instead — but there's no need to quote the rest of it, since these long quotes don't fool anybody." We've always remembered that professor, and wondered whatever became of him. Of course, we could pretend that he eventually moved to the Cayman Islands, which would tie up the end of this story rather neatly, but it wouldn't be strictly true. The whole story's pretty fishy already. Anyway, we're *not* still in college (for those of you who remember the beginning of this paragraph, and we're mighty grateful to you).

In the end, the better part of Mother's Day weekend was invested in this volume, we are proud to say. Upon finishing, one can wax philosophical and ask, "Why is a television star writing a book, anyway?" Well, why do authors keep popping up on TV, carrying their books (and often wearing jogging suits. Can anyone explain this?)?

Well, how about that? We just finished another chapter. Who said this book stuff was tough?

Thank you.

photo by Christopher L

"Pam, after she was told we needed ten thousand more words."